Bear-ly Bear-able

BEAR RIDDLES, JOKES, AND KNOCK-KNOCKS

Written and illustrated by MORT GERBERG

Featuring Riddle Bear

SCHOLASTIC INC.

New York Toronto London Auckland Sydney

For Cynthia

Other Scholastic books written and illustrated by Mort Gerberg

Computer Hooters!
Computer Riddles, Jokes and Knock-Knocks

Why Did Halley's Comet Cross the Universe?
And Other Riddles, Jokes, and Knock-Knocks

ISBN 0-590-40046-0

Copyright © 1987 by Mort Gerberg.
All rights reserved. Published by Scholastic Inc.
Art direction by Diana Hrisinko.

12 11 10 9 8 7 6 5 4   8 9/8 0 1 2/9

Printed in the U.S.A.   23
First Scholastic printing, September 1987

What color is a polar bear?
White.
Right. What color is a brown bear?
Brown.
Right. What color is a black bear?
Black.
Right. What color is a blue bear?
Blue.
Wrong. They don't come in that color.

Where do bears go when they want to take a bath?

To the bearthroom.

Where do bears go to get their hair cut?

To the bear-bear shop.

Why do bears climb up trees?

Because they can't fly.

Why do bears hibernate?

Because there's nothing good on television.

What time did Riddle Bear set his alarm for when he went to hibernate?

A quarter till spring.

What did
Riddle Bear say
when his mother
caught him with
his paw in the honey jar?

"Ooh, I'm so
embearassed."

Rena Bear: Hey, Riddle Bear, why are you humming?
Riddle Bear: I've joined a choir.
Rena Bear: Really?
        What kind of voice do you have?
Riddle Bear: Bear-it-tone.

Knock. Knock.
Who's there?
Bear watch.
Bear watch who?
Bear watch out, bear not cry, Bear not pout, I'm telling you why, Santa Claus is coming to town.

Knock. Knock.
Who's there?
Claws.
Claws who?
Claws the door, it's cold outside.

Knock. Knock.
Who's there?
Alaska Bear.
Alaska Bear who?
**Alaska Bear, but he may
not know the answer.**

Knock. Knock.
Who's there?
Fur.
Fur who?
**Fur he's a jolly good fellow,
Fur he's a jolly good fellow.**

**When can a polar bear
pick up water in his claws?**

When it's an ice cube.

**What would you call
a big tooth belonging
to a polar bear?**

A polar molar.

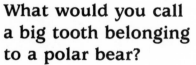

Why was the polar bear late for his appointment at the North Pole?

He had to keep stopping for the Northern Lights.

How can you get a bear to like you a lot?

Wear a lid on your head and act very, very sweet,
and he'll think you're a jar of honey.

Why does Riddle Bear take off his sneakers when he gets home?

He loves to walk around in his bear feet.

What did Riddle Bear take with him when he went for his skydiving lesson?

His bear-a-chute.

Which two kinds of bears have a lot to do with photography?

The Kodiak and the Polaroid.

Boy: How can you tell the difference between a real, live bear and a teddy bear?

Girl: If you have to ask, you'd better not hug it.

What kind of bear lives in the water, has a large mouthful of very sharp teeth, and is very ferocious?

The bear-a-cuda.

Famous Bears From History

Which English bear wrote plays that are the most well known in the English language?

William Shakesbear.

Which German bear wrote classical music, including nine symphonies?

Ludwig Van Bearthoven.

Which American bear was a catcher for the New York Yankees?

Yogi Beara.

Which Russian bear is a wonderful ballet dancer?

Mikhail Bearishnikov.

Which Italian bear is a great opera singer?

Luciano Bearvarotti.

Who was the most important person to Cinderella Bear?

Her beary godmother.

What has 14 legs, yellow and brown hair, and is found in the woods?

Goldilocks and the Three Bears.

Riddle Bear: Who wears a wide-brimmed hat and blue overalls, fights forest fires, and is brown and hairy?

Rena Bear: Smokey the Bear?

Riddle Bear: No, a suntanned forest ranger who hasn't shaved for a week.

Rena Bear: Who wears a wide-brimmed hat and blue overalls, fights forest fires, is brown and hairy, and has big ears?

Riddle Bear: Smokey the Bear?

Rena Bear: No, Smokey the *Hare*.

When he does magic tricks, what is the magic word
that Riddle Bear says to make something disappear?

A-bear-ca-da-bear!

Knock. Knock.
Who's there?
Bees.
Bees who?
Bees pass the honey.

Knock. Knock.
Who's there?
Koala.
Koala who?
**Koala for help—
the house is on fire!**

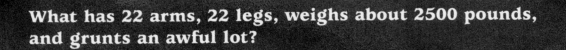

What has 22 arms, 22 legs, weighs about 2500 pounds, and grunts an awful lot?

The Chicago Bears football team.

Why do grizzly bears live in caves?

They can't afford apartments in the city.

Which bear goes around finding fault with everything?

Winnie the Pooh-Pooh.

Which bear goes around trying to scare everybody?

Winnie the Booh!

Which bear goes around doing imitations of cows?

Winnie the Mooh.

Mrs. Bear: My husband, Bernie Bear, has gone a little crazy.

Mrs. Rabbit: What do you mean?

Mrs. Bear: Well, he thinks he's a beehive, and he keeps buzzing around all day.

Mrs. Rabbit: Goodness, did you take him to the doctor?

Mrs. Bear: We're thinking about it, but he makes such good honey.

Riddle Bear climbed up a tall pine tree to gather
some acorns for his lunch, but though he tried all morning,
he couldn't get any. Why not?

Acorns don't grow on pine trees; they grow on oak trees.

Where do many bears go for their winter vacations?

To Bear-muda.

Where do bears who are in the army live?

In bear-acks.

Why was the 12-year-old Jewish bear singing in Hebrew?

He was practicing for his bear-mitzvah.

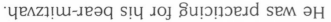

Why is a blushing panda like a newspaper?

They're both black and white and red (read) all over.

The forest ranger tried to get into his lookout station,
but it was locked, and he didn't have his keys with him.
How did he open the door?

He used Smokey's.

What would you think if a ferocious grizzly bear suddenly rushed up to you, threw his arms around you, and started to crush you in a bear hug?

That he was very, very glad to see you.

What would you call a white bear
who loves to lie in the sun?

A solar polar.

What would you call a white bear who loves to lie in the sun
and listen to popular music?

A solar rock 'n roller polar.

What would you call a white bear who loves to lie in the sun
and listen to popular music and roll a black ball at wooden clubs?

A solar rock 'n roller bowler polar.

What would you call a white bear who loves to lie in the sun and listen
to popular music and roll a black ball at wooden clubs
while drinking soda?

A solar rock 'n roller bowler cola polar.

What is this a picture of?

A bear-el of fun.